JUL 2 1 2008

Electric Guitar Man

The Genius of Les Paul

Edwin Brit Wyckoff

Enslow Elementary

an imprint of

Enslow Publishers, Inc.
40 Industrial Road
Box 398
Berkeley Heights, NJ 07922
USA

http://www.enslow.com

Content Adviser

Burton W. Peretti, Ph.D.
Music Historian
Chair, Department of History and Non-Western Cultures
Western Connecticut State University

Series Literacy Consultant

Allan A. De Fina, Ph.D.
Past President of the New Jersey Reading Association
Chairperson, Department of Literacy Education
New Jersey City University

Enslow Elementary, an imprint of Enslow Publishers, Inc.

Enslow Elementary® is a registered trademark of Enslow Publishers, Inc.

Library of Congress Cataloging-in-Publication Data

Wyckoff, Edwin Brit.
    Electric guitar man: the genius of Les Paul / by Edwin Brit Wyckoff.
        p. cm.—(Genius at work! great inventor biographies)
    Includes bibliographical references and index.
    ISBN-13: 978-0-7660-2847-0
    ISBN-10: 0-7660-2847-X
    1. Paul, Les—Juvenile literature. 2. Guitarists—United States—Biography—Juvenile literature.
    3. Inventors—United States—Biography—Juvenile literature. I. Title.
    ML3930.P29W93 2007
    781.64092—dc22
    [B]
                                                            2006034681

Printed in the United States of America

10 9 8 7 6 5 4 3 2 1

To Our Readers:
We have done our best to make sure all Internet Addresses in this book were active and appropriate when we went to press. However, the author and the publisher have no control over and assume no liability for the material available on those Internet sites or on other Web sites they may link to. Any comments or suggestions can be sent by e-mail to comments@enslow.com or to the address on the back cover.

Photo Credits: © 1999, Artville, LLC, p. 4; © 2007 Jupiterimages Corporation, pp. 1 (left), 17 (center, left); Associated Press, pp. 22, 23, 27, 28; Chris Walter/WireImage/Getty Images, pp. 3 (inset), 24; Courtesy of Nashville Country Music Foundation, p. 12; Courtesy Russ Cochran/Photo by Wolf Hoffman, p. 11; © Enslow Publishers, Inc., p. 3 (background); Fred Waring's America (Pennsylvania State University), p. 14; Hulton Archive/Getty Images, p. 10; Giuseppe Cacace/Getty Images, p. 26; ©iStockphoto.com/Gilbert Muro, p. 7; mando maniac, p. 19; Michael Ochs Archives/Getty Images, pp. 1 (right), 18; Photofest, pp. 8, 13, 21; Photograph by John Peden, Courtesy of Lemelson Center, Smithsonian Institution, p. 17 (right); Shutterstock, pp. 5, 11; Waukesha County Historical Society and Museum, pp. 4 (inset), 6.

Front Cover Photos: Associated Press (inset); Ralph Notaro/Getty Images (background)

Back Cover Photo: © 2007 Jupiterimages Corporation

Contents

1   The Bubbling, Boiling Harmonica 5

2   Red Hot Red 10

3   Night and Day 15

4   Sound-on-Sound 19

5   Monday Night Madness 25

Timeline 29

Words to Know 30

Learn More

    Books and Internet Addresses 31

Index 32

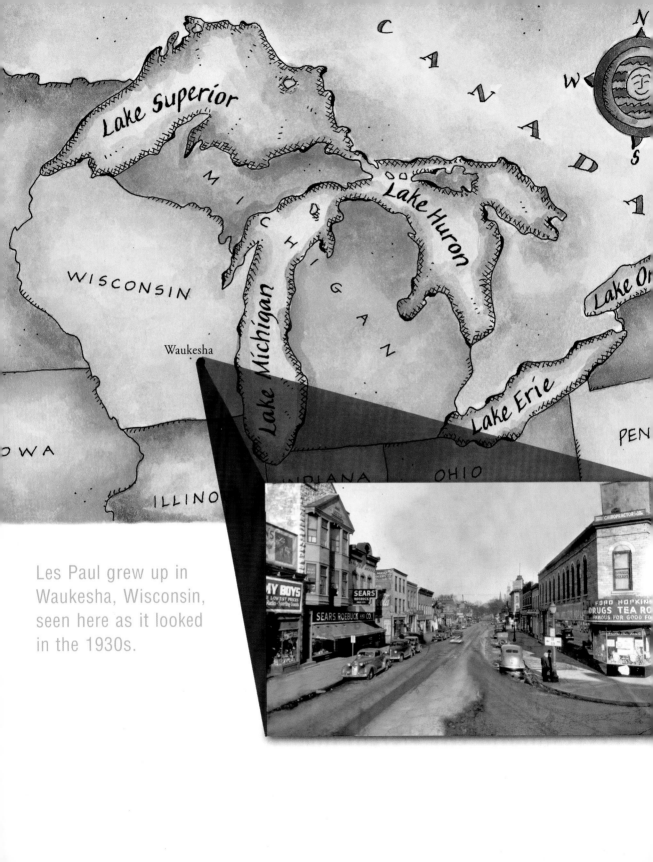

Les Paul grew up in Waukesha, Wisconsin, seen here as it looked in the 1930s.

Chapter 1

The Bubbling, Boiling Harmonica

Some summer days are so hot there is nothing to do but sit and watch the clouds drift by. So on one such day in 1923, eight-year-old Les Polsfuss did just that. As he sat in front of his house in Waukesha, Wisconsin, a man dug a ditch in the street. Eventually the tired man sat down on the edge of the ditch. He wiped his face with a bright kerchief. Then he began to play tunes on a harmonica.

Les crept closer and closer to see how the man's hands held the instrument. Finally the man stopped, looked at Les, and offered him the harmonica. The shy boy shook his

A harmonica

Les (right) with his older brother, Ralph

head to say no. The man blurted out, "Don't say you can't . . . until you've proved you can't!" He shoved the harmonica into the boy's hands and walked off.

Les went home holding the old, dirty instrument. His mother grabbed it, raced to the kitchen, and boiled it clean in a pot of bubbling water. Only then did she let her son use it. Soon, Les taught himself to play the harmonica along with music on the radio.

Lester William Polsfuss was born in Waukesha, Wisconsin, on June 9, 1915. His father, George Polsfuss, was a very smart businessman.

Les's mother, Evelyn, was a woman with very strong opinions about everything. She thought Les was a musical genius. His older brother, Ralph, didn't care much about music. So Les was the star of the family.

When he was nine, Les thought a lot about taking apart his mother's player piano. She told him not to fool with it. That was like putting cheese in a mousetrap and telling the mouse to leave it alone. Secretly, Les took apart the gears, the foot pump, and the rolls of punched paper that worked the piano keys. He punched new holes in the

As a child, Les took apart a player piano.

Les could play the guitar and the harmonica at the same time.

paper to make new music. And he put the piano back together again.

Les got his first guitar at age eleven. He rigged up a wire coat hanger to curve around his neck and hold the harmonica close to his mouth. Then he invented a way to flip the harmonica with his chin so he could get different sounds from each side. His hands were free to play the guitar. Les was a walking, talking, singing, one-man band.

Chapter 2

Red Hot Red

When he was just thirteen, the kid with fire-engine-red hair started raking in money with his one-man band. He played and sang outside the busiest drive-in restaurant in town. They served barbecued ribs and chicken.

Les's one-man band was a hit in his hometown of Waukesha.

Les served up great country music. One driver who rolled by yelled that the guitar had to be louder. Les listened.

The young inventor went back to work. He took one radio from his mother and one from his father to use as loudspeakers. He took apart a telephone to get its

Les was always trying to find a better sound using electricity. For one experiment, Les lugged home a fifty-pound section of steel railroad track. He put a couple of railroad spikes across the track. Then he stretched a wire across the track from end to end.

Next, he put a microphone he had taken out of a telephone under the wire. He plucked his one-string steel "guitar," and the sound was perfect. There was no feedback, or squeaks and squeals that often come from electrified guitars. He had found the one perfect note of music he would remember the rest of his life.

microphone. He hooked the whole thing right into the guitar. Then he plugged his invention into electricity from the restaurant. Tips poured in. But when there was a prizefight on the radio, or a concert his mother wanted to hear, his parents took back their radios. Les was out of making money for the day. That was no way to run a business.

"Pie Plant Pete's" real name was Claude Moye.

Les's mother took her young genius to theaters to see great guitar players like "Pie Plant Pete." Pete played wild country music, sang, and told funny stories. Evelyn took Les backstage. Pete showed him a few guitar tricks. Les picked up the tricks, practiced them overnight, and came back for more the next day. His playing got so "hot" that his mother started calling him "Red Hot Red." Evelyn came up with a slogan, "Music So Rotten . . . It's Good." But Les's music wasn't rotten. It was beginning to be great.

Les met another fantastic guitar player named "Sunny" Joe Wolverton. Joe was twenty-five. Les was only sixteen, but his mother let him leave school and go on the road with "Sunny" Joe. Les was reborn as "Rhubarb Red."

The pair played at dance clubs, theaters, and radio stations all over the Midwest. One day, "Sunny" decided that he wanted to see Australia. Les wanted to work in the United States, so they split up. Lester changed his name to Les Paul. He was a lone guitarist, looking for work.

When he played with "Sunny" Joe, Les (right) took on the name "Rhubarb Red."

The Les Paul Trio (Les Paul, left) with Fred Waring (right) and singer Donna Dae.

Chapter 3

Night and Day

Les loved to work. Always looking for jobs, he boasted, "I tell jokes, I play the piano, the guitar, the harmonica, the banjo, and the jug. I sweep. I cook. I do anything to work." That included playing at radio stations and clubs and working on inventions all night long.

In 1937, Les met and married Virginia Webb. In 1938, Les put together the "Les Paul Trio," and they headed for New York City. Les had bragged that he was a good friend of Paul Whiteman, one of the big-name bandleaders in the country. Actually, Whiteman did not know Les. When the trio went to see Whiteman, he chased them out of his office and slammed the door.

As they waited sadly for the elevator to take them back down, Les spotted Fred Waring, another big time bandleader. Les asked if they could play for Waring in the elevator. The boys played fast. Waring listened fast and hired them fast. The trio was featured on the much-loved "Fred Waring and His Pennsylvanians" show for years.

Les was becoming two people. One was a great guitarist who told funny, corny jokes. The second Les Paul was an inventor. He designed hollow-body and solid-body guitars. They both could be electrified to send waves of music out to the audience. But they tended to make screechy feedback noises. Les was still searching for that solid sound he had heard on his railroad track guitar.

For hundreds of years, guitars were designed with hollow bodies, the same way that violins are hollow inside.

Solid body guitars became popular with rock and roll. They are made of thick wood. They depend on electric amplifiers to carry their sounds.

In 1941, Les put strings on a four-by-four block of solid wood. Then he cut a guitar into two halves and stuck them on the heavy wood. With great pride he took the strange-looking thing to the powerful Gibson Guitar Corporation. They nearly laughed Les and "The Log" out of their offices. Later they would beg him to come back.

a hollow-body guitar

"The Log" was Les Paul's most famous early attempt at making a solid-body guitar.

a solid-body guitar

Les Paul created a new sound by experimenting with layers of sound.

Chapter 4

Sound-on-Sound

By 1943, Les Paul was the top guitarist in the country. Soon he had his dream job working with the famous singer Bing Crosby. Les was inventing new ways to record music at different speeds. Crosby bought expensive tape recorders to help Les invent something new.

His mom called him on the phone. She said, "You're great, but you sound like everyone else." Evelyn was tough, but she was right. So Les invented something he called sound-on-sound. One layer of music was recorded over another layer. Each

The cover of one of Les Paul's records, *The New Sound!*

layer was a little bit different. Sometimes the final recording had as many as eight layers of sound. Nobody had ever heard music like that before, because it had never been done before. Les also learned how to add an echo, so that music bounced at listeners as though they were inside the guitar.

Les needed one more sound. It turned out to be Iris Colleen Summers. She had a great voice, played the guitar well, and was wonderful with audiences. Les changed her name to Mary Ford, and the two went on to make history. They won thirteen gold records, which meant that each record sold more than a million copies. Les and Mary raced wildly from city to city by car entertaining cheering audiences.

On January 26, 1948, their world turned upside down. Their high-powered car smashed off the highway. Six of Les's ribs were broken. His

Les Paul and Mary Ford recorded many songs using sound-on-sound and other new sound effects.

playing arm was shattered. After six months with his arm in a plaster cast, Les had to learn how to play the guitar all over again.

Les had stopped long enough to realize that he loved Mary. He and Virginia divorced in 1949. In December of the same year, Les and Mary got married. The couple's new recordings soared right back to the top of the record charts.

In 1951, they sold four million records. That year, they made $20,000 a week, which would be equal to about $100,000 a week today.

Gibson Guitar came back to Les in 1952. The company finally wanted a solid-body electric guitar. The "Les Paul"

Gibson Guitar decided to start selling Les Paul's guitars in 1952.

design became a best-seller. It was like having the "Log" come back to life.

In just eleven months, Les and Mary had seven hit songs and sold over 6 million records. Their television show, "The Les Paul and Mary Ford at Home Show," went on the air in October 1953 and ran until 1960. The President of the United States, Dwight Eisenhower, asked them to play at the White House in Washington, D.C.

Mary almost cried when she heard about the invitation. "No," she said, "there's just too much work." Les could never say no. Mary went along but their marriage was over. They divorced in 1964. "Red Hot Red" was cooling down. He was only forty-nine, but he was rich. So he stopped working.

Les and Mary recorded their television show at their home in Oakland, New Jersey.

Les went back to work after his mother told him to "Get with it!"

Chapter 5

Monday Night Madness

Les's mother waited and waited for Les to go back to work. Finally she phoned. "Get with it!" she told him. "Get with it!" He had been slipping out of sight of his fans for years. Then, in 1984, he formed a new Les Paul Trio. He got back to work.

The trio took over Monday nights at clubs in New York City. Ever since, fans pile into an underground club called the Iridium Jazz Club, which is near the bright lights of Times Square. Lots of them come carrying guitars that Les will sign for them as they stay until one or two in the morning. He hates going to bed before dawn.

Great musicians come to see Les because he jazzed up jazz, he put sparkle into country music, and he rocked long before there was rock and roll.

The Log—It looked strange, but the solid wood block produced a great sound with none of the squeals and noises of feedback.

Sound-on-sound—Recording layer over layer of music and voices to make them sound like an orchestra and choir. It is also called overdubbing or multi-dubbing.

Echo chambers—Sound is pumped into a specially designed room so that it bounces back again and again. You can produce the same effect by singing while walking through a tunnel.

The Les Paul Paulverizer—A secret electronic box Les kept backstage at live concerts. He could produce sound-on-sound, echoes, and sound effects backing up the live performers. The audience saw one or two people, but it sounded like many more.

Gibson Les Paul Guitar—The shape, the thickness, the paint, the length of the neck, and the way the strings were stretched were exactly what Les wanted. Many professional guitarists have at least one Gibson Les Paul guitar. Some of the early models are worth thousands of dollars.

Many professional guitarists, like Lenny Kravitz, use Gibson Les Paul guitars.

In 1988, Les was inducted into the Rock-and-Roll Hall of Fame. He was also voted into the National Inventors Hall of Fame in 2005.

Les had shown the music world how to put layers of sound on sound. He came up with new ways of changing speeds on his recordings tracks, creating more new sounds. A top guitarist wrote that without Les Paul, there would have been no

Les plays for his fans every Monday night at the Iridium Jazz Club in New York City.

Jimi Hendrix, no Jeff Beck, no Jimmy Page, no Pink Floyd, no U2, no Beatles.

In 2007 at the age of 92, Les Paul was still going strong. His fingers had become stiff with a painful disease called arthritis, but he was happy entertaining his fans. He continued to tell good old jokes, get off "hot licks" on his guitar, and have fun with guests from around the world.

One of the Beatles, Paul McCartney, once said "I visited him in New York . . . the magic is still there." McCartney went on, "The new ideas he brought to the electric guitar are astounding . . . Les is truly one of the greats."

In 2007, Les Paul received the National Medal of Arts from President George W. Bush.

1915	Born in Waukesha, Wisconsin, on June 9.
1932	Joins "Sunny" Joe Wolverton in a two-man band playing at Midwest radio stations and clubs.
1937	Marries Virginia Webb. They later have two sons.
1938	"The Les Paul Trio" is hired to become a featured act on Fred Waring's national radio show.
1943	Moves to Hollywood, California. Experiments with recording music in his home recording studio.
1946	Starts recording songs with Mary Ford. Their layered sound-on-sound style becomes popular.
1948	Playing arm is shattered in a serious car accident. Has to learn how to play guitar all over again.
1949	Divorces Virginia. Marries Mary Ford on December 29. They later adopt a girl and have a son.
1952	Develops the Gibson Les Paul Guitar, still one of the most famous electric guitars today.
1964	Les and Mary divorce. Les retires.
1984	Starts playing at a music club in New York City every Monday night.
1988	Is inducted into the Rock and Roll Hall of Fame.
2005	Is inducted into the National Inventors Hall of Fame.
2007	Receives National Medal of Arts.

acoustic guitar—A hollow-body guitar that does not need to use electricity to make its sound heard.

amplifier—An electronic system that makes sounds louder. It can control and change the sound.

arthritis—A disease which makes fingers and other joints swollen and stiff. It can be very painful.

feedback—Nasty squeaks and squeals often caused by electrically amplified musical instruments.

inducted—To be accepted into a club or honorary society.

jazz—American music with rich harmony and a driving rhythm.

player piano—A mechanical piano which uses a punched paper roll to pick out the notes for the music.

record chart—A list of the most popular music recordings.

sound effects—The sound such as a train, rain, thunder, cannon, fire, or wind, used in films or music.

trio—A group of three people such as musicians.

Books

Bay, William. *Mel Bay Presents: Children's Guitar Chord Book*. Pacific, Mo.: Mel Bay, 2000.

Macaulay, David. *The New Way Things Work*. Boston: Houghton Mifflin, 1998.

Scholastic Books, ed. *Musical Instruments: From Flutes Carved of Bone, to Lutes, to Modern Electric Guitars*. New York: Scholastic, 1994.

Internet Addresses

ZOOM by Kids, for Kids! Build Your Own Guitar.
http://pbskids.org/zoom/activities/sci/guitar.html

Science News For Kids: Extra Strings for New Sounds.
http://www.sciencenewsforkids.org/articles/20060607/Note3.asp

A

arthritis, 28

C

car accident, 20–22, 29
coat wire invention, 9
Crosby, Bing, 19

E

echoes, 20, 26
Eisenhower, Dwight, 23
electricity, in guitars, 10–11, 16

F

Ford, Mary, 20, 22, 23, 29

G

Gibson Guitar Corporation, 17, 22
Gibson Les Paul Guitar, 22–23, 26, 29
gold records, 20
guitars. *See also* Log, the.
    experiments with, 9, 16
    hollow-body, 16, 17
    as one-man band, 10–11
    relearning, after car accident, 20–22, 29
    solid-body, 16, 17

H

harmonicas, 5–6, 9
hit songs, 23

I

inventions, list of, 26
Iridium Jazz Club, 25

L

Les Paul Gibson Guitar, 22–23, 26, 29
Les Paul Paulverizer, 26
Les Paul Trio, 15–16, 25, 29
Log, the, 17, 23, 26
loudspeakers, 10–11

M

music recording experiments, 19, 29
    layered style of, 19–20, 26, 29

N

name change, 13
New York City, 15, 25, 29

O

one-man band, 10–11

P

Paul, Les
    birth, 6, 29
    children, 29
    divorces, 22, 23, 29
    legacy, 26–28

marriages, 22, 29
    retirement, 29
"Pie Plant Pete," 12
player piano, 7–9
Polsfuss, Evelyn (mother), 6, 7, 12, 19, 25
Polsfuss, George (father), 6
Polsfuss, Lester William. *See* Paul, Les.
Polsfuss, Ralph (brother), 6, 7

R

record sales, 22
"Red Hot Red," 12, 23
"Rhubarb Red," 12, 13

S

salary, 22
sound experiments, 10–11
sound-on-sound style, 19–20, 26, 29
Summers, Iris Colleen. *See* Ford, Mary.

T

television career, 23

W

Waring, Fred, 16
Washington, D.C., 23
Webb, Virginia, 15, 22, 29
Whiteman, Paul, 15–16
Wolverton, "Sunny" Joe, 12–13, 29